Military Tracked Vehicles

by Grace Hansen

Abdo
MILITARY AIRCRAFT & VEHICLES
Kids

abdopublishing.com

Published by Abdo Kids, a division of ABDO, PO Box 398166, Minneapolis, Minnesota 55439.

Copyright © 2017 by Abdo Consulting Group, Inc. International copyrights reserved in all countries. No part of this book may be reproduced in any form without written permission from the publisher.

Printed in the United States of America, North Mankato, Minnesota.

102016

012017

Photo Credits: Images of Freedom, iStock, marines.mil, Shutterstock ©PhotoStock10 p.cover / Shutterstock.com, ©The U.S. Army p.5, 7 / CC-BY-2.0

Production Contributors: Teddy Borth, Jennie Forsberg, Grace Hansen

Design Contributors: Laura Mitchell, Dorothy Toth

Publisher's Cataloging in Publication Data

Names: Hansen, Grace, author.

Title: Military tracked vehicles / by Grace Hansen.

Description: Minneapolis, Minnesota : Abdo Kids, 2017 | Series: Military aircraft & vehicles | Includes bibliographical references and index.

Identifiers: LCCN 2016944107 | ISBN 9781680809367 (lib. bdg.) | ISBN 9781680796469 (ebook) | ISBN 9781680797138 (Read-to-me ebook)

Subjects: LCSH: Vehicles, Military--Juvenile literature. | Tanks (Military science)--Juvenile literature. | Armored vehicles, Military--Juvenile literature.

Classification: DDC 623.7/475--dc23

LC record available at http://lccn.loc.gov/2016944107

Table of Contents

Tracks!

Militaries use tracked vehicles.

Tracks help giant tanks move

and not get stuck.

BFV

The **BFV** is an armored fighting vehicle. Its main job is to safely move troops. Its other job is to give covering fire.

6

The Bradley M2 carries three crewmembers. They are the commander, gunner, and driver. It also carries six **infantrymen**.

9

Abrams

The Abrams is a main battle tank. It is very powerful.

Abrams tanks are made
of layers of steel and
other materials. They
are very hard to destroy.

The Abrams moves easily over many **terrains**. It is well armed. It is the best vehicle for the front lines.

15

Paladin

Paladins are like tanks.

But they have larger

cannons and thinner armor.

Paladins have an important job. It is to support **infantry** and tanks on the battlefield.

The Paladin's main weapon is the M284 155mm howitzer. It is a cannon. It can fire four rounds per minute. It can hit targets up to 18.6 miles (30 km) away!

The Abrams Tank Up Close

- Crew: 4

- Cruising range: 265 miles (426 km)

- Maximum speed: 42 mph (68 km/h)

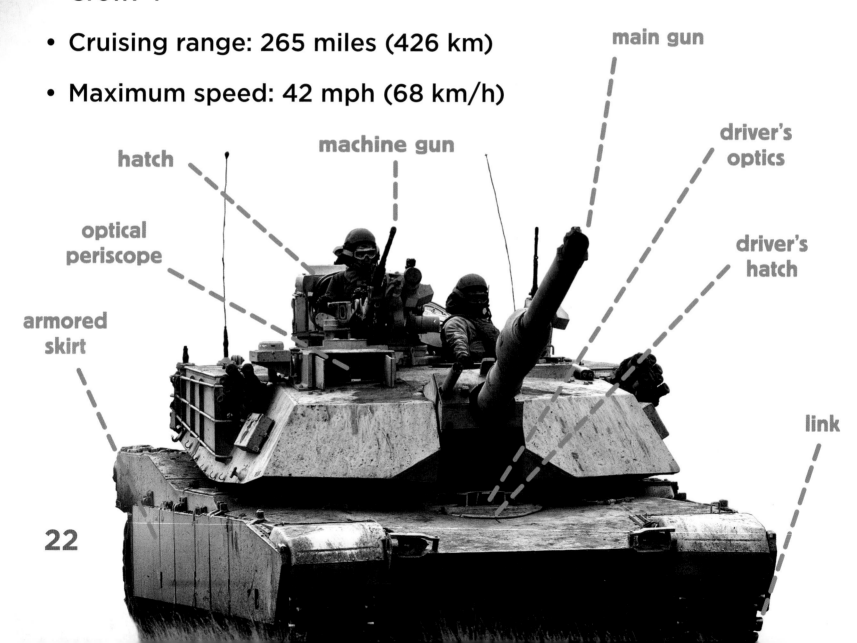

main gun

driver's optics

machine gun

driver's hatch

hatch

optical periscope

armored skirt

link

Glossary

BFV – Bradley Fighting Vehicle.

infantry – the part of an army that has soliders who fight on foot.

infantrymen – soldiers who are in the infantry.

terrain – a stretch of land, especially with regard to its physical features.

Index

abdokids.com

Use this code to log on to abdokids.com and access crafts, games, videos, and more!

Abdo Kids Code:
MMK9367

24